BY LARRY MACK

THE DALLAS
COWBOYS
STORY

BELLWETHER MEDIA · MINNEAPOLIS, MN

Are you ready to take it to the extreme? Torque books thrust you into the action-packed world of sports, vehicles, mystery, and adventure. These books may include dirt, smoke, fire, and chilling tales. **WARNING**: read at your own risk.

This edition first published in 2017 by Bellwether Media, Inc.

No part of this publication may be reproduced in whole or in part without written permission of the publisher. For information regarding permission, write to Bellwether Media, Inc., Attention: Permissions Department, 5357 Penn Avenue South, Minneapolis, MN 55419.

Library of Congress Cataloging-in-Publication Data .

Names: Mack, Larry.
Title: The Dallas Cowboys Story / by Larry Mack.
Description: Minneapolis, MN : Bellwether Media, Inc., 2017. | Series:
   Torque: NFL teams | Includes bibliographical references and index.
Identifiers: LCCN 2015034275 | ISBN 9781626173637 (hardcover : alk. paper)
Subjects: LCSH: Dallas Cowboys (Football team)–History–Juvenile literature.
Classification: LCC GV956.D3 M32 2017 | DDC 796.332/64097642812–dc23
LC record available at https://lccn.loc.gov/2015034275

Printed in the United States of America, North Mankato, MN.

TABLE OF CONTENTS

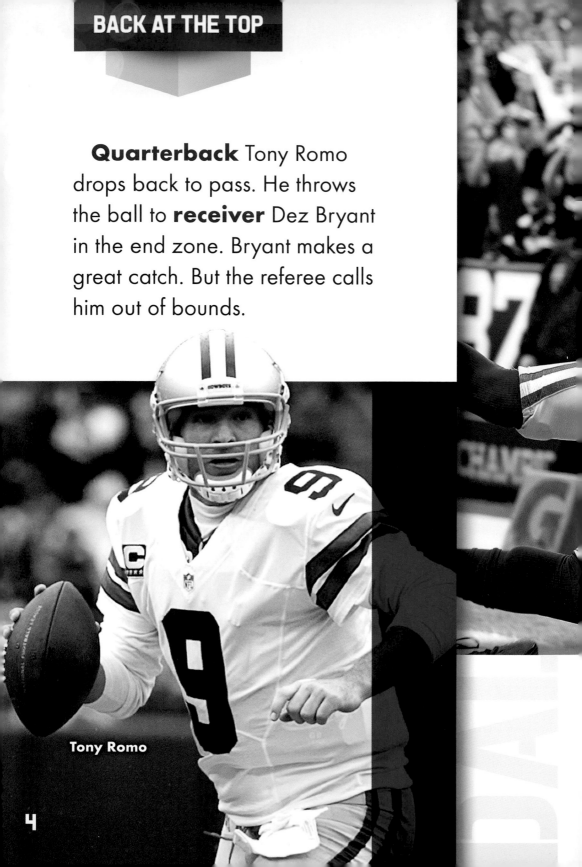

Quarterback Tony Romo drops back to pass. He throws the ball to **receiver** Dez Bryant in the end zone. Bryant makes a great catch. But the referee calls him out of bounds.

Tony Romo

Dez Bryant

The officials watch the replay. Bryant was in bounds. The Dallas Cowboys increase their lead over the Washington Redskins by a touchdown!

PLAYOFF-BOUND
The Dallas Cowboys have reached the National Football League (NFL) playoffs more than 30 times!

The scoreboard reads 44 to 17 as the final seconds tick off the game clock. The Cowboys give high fives. They have finished the 2014 regular season with a win. Now to the **playoffs**!

SCORING TERMS

END ZONE
the area at each end of a football field; a team scores by entering the opponent's end zone with the football.

EXTRA POINT
a score that occurs when a kicker kicks the ball between the opponent's goal posts after a touchdown is scored; 1 point.

FIELD GOAL
a score that occurs when a kicker kicks the ball between the opponent's goal posts; 3 points.

SAFETY
a score that occurs when a player on offense is tackled behind his own goal line; 2 points for defense.

TOUCHDOWN
a score that occurs when a team crosses into its opponent's end zone with the football; 6 points.

TWO-POINT CONVERSION
a score that occurs when a team crosses into its opponent's end zone with the football after scoring a touchdown; 2 points.

The Dallas Cowboys are one of the most successful teams in NFL history. They became known as "America's Team" in the 1970s.

VALUABLE TEAM
The Cowboys are one of the most valuable sports teams in the world. They are worth about $4 billion.

The team won the **Super Bowl** twice that decade. Suddenly their popularity soared. Then the 1990s brought more championships.

The Cowboys play in AT&T Stadium in Arlington, Texas. This is one of the NFL's newest stadiums. Its roof opens and closes. It also has huge video screens. The main screen is bigger than a basketball court!

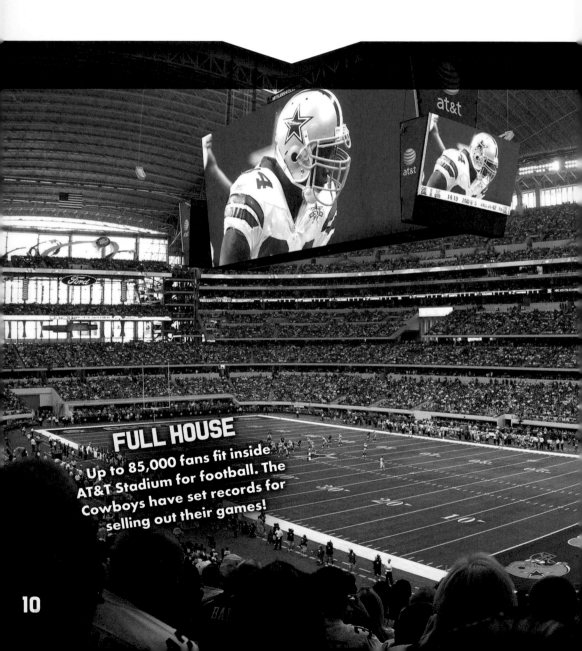

FULL HOUSE

Up to 85,000 fans fit inside AT&T Stadium for football. The Cowboys have set records for selling out their games!

AT&T STADIUM

ARLINGTON,
TEXAS

N
W E
S

There are 32 teams in the NFL. They are divided into two **conferences**.

The Cowboys are in the East **Division** of the National Football Conference (NFC) with the New York Giants, Philadelphia Eagles, and Washington Redskins. These teams are big **rivals**.

NFL DIVISIONS

AFC NORTH

 BALTIMORE **RAVENS**

CINCINNATI **BENGALS**

 CLEVELAND **BROWNS**

PITTSBURGH **STEELERS**

AFC EAST

 BUFFALO **BILLS**

 MIAMI **DOLPHINS**

 PATRIOTS

 NEW YORK **JETS**

AFC SOUTH

 TEXANS

 INDIANAPOLIS **COLTS**

 JACKSONVILLE **JAGUARS**

 TENNESSEE **TITANS**

AFC WEST

 DENVER **BRONCOS**

 CHIEFS

 OAKLAND **RAIDERS**

 SAN DIEGO **CHARGERS**

NFC

NFC NORTH

 CHICAGO **BEARS**

 DETROIT **LIONS**

 GREEN BAY **PACKERS**

 MINNESOTA **VIKINGS**

NFC EAST

 DALLAS **COWBOYS**

GIANTS

 PHILADELPHIA **EAGLES**

 WASHINGTON **REDSKINS**

NFC SOUTH

 FALCONS

 CAROLINA **PANTHERS**

NEW ORLEANS **SAINTS**

 BUCCANEERS

NFC WEST

 CARDINALS

 LOS ANGELES **RAMS**

 SAN FRANCISCO **49ERS**

 SEATTLE **SEAHAWKS**

The Cowboys entered the NFL in 1960. Tom Landry was their first coach. He led the team to their first **winning record** in 1966.

Then Landry guided the Cowboys to Super Bowl wins in 1972 and 1978. He coached the Cowboys for a record 29 seasons in a row!

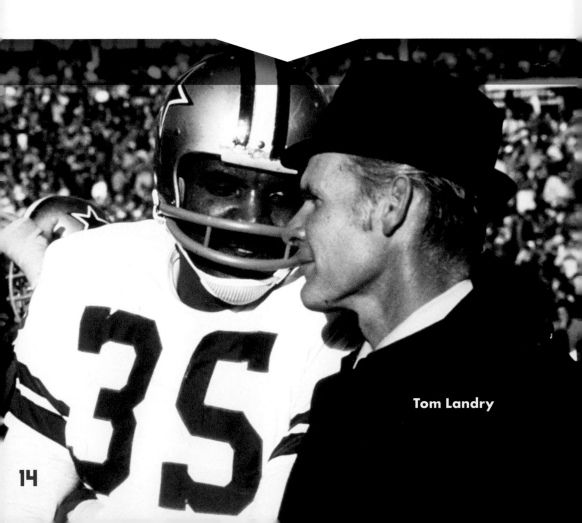

Tom Landry

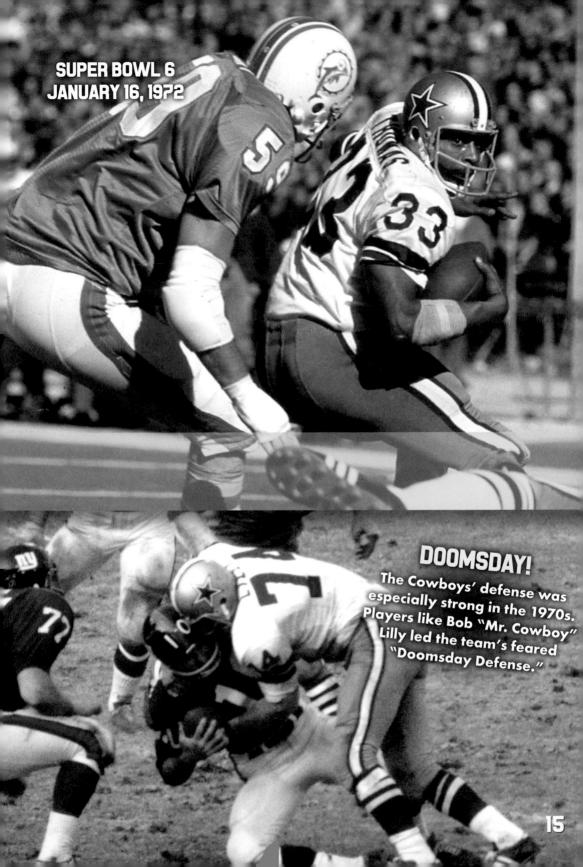

DOOMSDAY!

The Cowboys' defense was especially strong in the 1970s. Players like Bob "Mr. Cowboy" Lilly led the team's feared "Doomsday Defense."

In 1989, Jerry Jones bought the Cowboys. The team had gone through a few bad seasons. Jones replaced Landry with Jimmy Johnson.

Jimmy Johnson

Jerry Jones

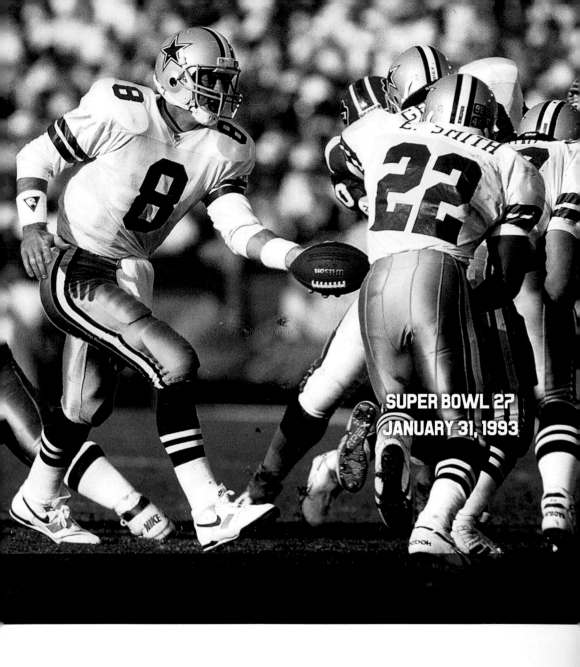

SUPER BOWL 27
JANUARY 31, 1993

The new coach led the team back to the top of the NFL. They won Super Bowl 27 in 1993. Since the late 1990s, the Cowboys have been hungry for another Super Bowl win.

COWBOYS
TIMELINE

1978
Won Super Bowl 12, beating the Denver Broncos

27 FINAL SCORE **10**

1960
Approved as a new team by the NFL

1972
Won Super Bowl 6, beating the Miami Dolphins

24 FINAL SCORE **3**

1989
Purchased by Jerry Jones

1993

Won Super Bowl 27, beating the Buffalo Bills

52 FINAL SCORE **17**

1994

Won Super Bowl 28, beating the Buffalo Bills

30 FINAL SCORE **13**

2002

Celebrated Emmitt Smith breaking the NFL record for most career rushing yards

2014

Claimed first NFC East title since 2009

1996

Won Super Bowl 30, beating the Pittsburgh Steelers

27 FINAL SCORE **17**

2009

Played first regular season game at new Cowboys Stadium

The Cowboys have had many talented quarterbacks lead their **offense**. Roger Staubach helped Dallas win Super Bowl 12 in 1978.

Roger Staubach

Troy Aikman

Tony Romo

In 1989, Troy Aikman joined the Cowboys. He started his career with 11 losses but became an NFL great. Today, the team's star quarterback is Tony Romo.

Running back Tony Dorsett helped the Cowboys win Super Bowl 12. He was only a **rookie** at the time. Some say Emmitt Smith was the greatest running back ever. He **rushed** for 17,162 yards with the Cowboys.

Today, **tight end** Jason Witten is a star. He has been to the **Pro Bowl** ten times already.

TEAM GREATS

BOB LILLY
DEFENSIVE TACKLE
1961-1974

ROGER STAUBACH
QUARTERBACK
1969-1979

TONY DORSETT
RUNNING BACK
1977-1987

Jason Witten

TROY AIKMAN
QUARTERBACK
1989-2000

EMMITT SMITH
RUNNING BACK
1990-2002

JASON WITTEN
TIGHT END
2003-PRESENT

The Cowboys have fans all over the United States. Some of these fans are Texans who moved away from home. But the team's many playoff appearances and several Super Bowls have also helped the team win fans!

COWBOYS CO-STARS
The Dallas Cowboys Cheerleaders are almost as famous as the football team. They even have their own reality TV show!

The Cowboys hold one of the longest traditions in the NFL. Almost every year since 1966, they have played on Thanksgiving Day.

**THANKSGIVING DAY GAME
NOVEMBER 26, 2015**

Another tradition is always wearing their white jerseys at home games. In white or blue, the Dallas Cowboys are sure to remain America's Team!

MORE ABOUT THE
COWBOYS

Team name:
Dallas Cowboys

Team name explained:
Named after men
who take care of
cattle on ranches

Nickname:
America's Team

Joined NFL: 1960

Conference: NFC

Division: East

**Main rivals: New York Giants,
Washington Redskins**

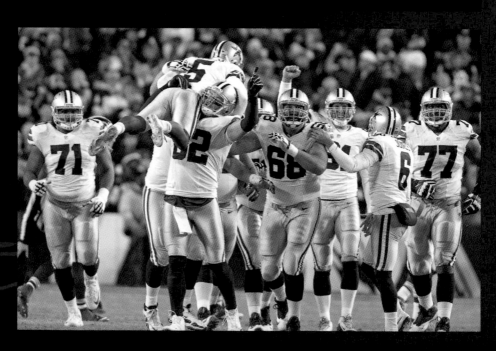

Hometown:
Dallas, Texas

Training camp location:
River Ridge Playing Fields, Oxnard, California

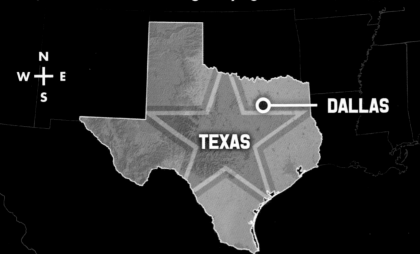

DALLAS

TEXAS

Home stadium name: AT&T Stadium
(formerly called Cowboys Stadium)

Stadium opened: 2009

Seats in stadium: 85,000

Logo: Blue star, which
represents Texas, or
the "Lone Star State"

Colors: Silver, white,
blue (navy and royal)

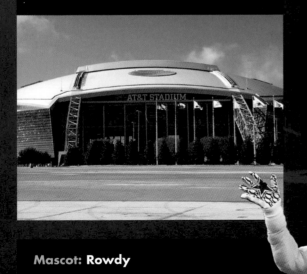

Mascot: Rowdy

GLOSSARY

conferences—large groupings of sports teams that often play one another

division—a small grouping of sports teams that often play one another; usually there are several divisions of teams in a conference.

offense—the group of players who try to move down the field and score

playoffs—the games played after the regular NFL season is over; playoff games determine which teams play in the Super Bowl.

Pro Bowl—an all-star game played after the regular season in which the best players in the NFL face one another

quarterback—a player on offense whose main job is to throw and hand off the ball

receiver—a player on offense whose main job is to catch passes from the quarterback

rivals—teams that are long-standing opponents

rookie—a first-year player in a sports league

running back—a player on offense whose main job is to run with the ball

rushed—ran with the ball to gain yards

Super Bowl—the championship game for the NFL

tight end—a player on offense whose main jobs are to catch the ball and block for teammates

winning record—when a team has more wins than losses in a season

TO LEARN MORE

AT THE LIBRARY

Frisch, Aaron. *Dallas Cowboys*. Mankato, Minn.: Creative Education, 2014.

Wyner, Zach. *Dallas Cowboys*. New York, N.Y.: AV2 by Weigl, 2015.

Zappa, Marcia. *Dallas Cowboys*. Edina, Minn.: ABDO Pub. Company, 2015.

ON THE WEB

Learning more about the
Dallas Cowboys is as
easy as 1, 2, 3.

1. Go to www.factsurfer.com.

2. Enter "Dallas Cowboys" into the search box.

3. Click the "Surf" button and you will see a list of
related web sites.

With factsurfer.com, finding more
information is just a click away.

INDEX